PUFFIN POETRY

GARGLING
with Jelly

BRIAN PATTEN was born in Liverpool. His poetry
for adults has been translated into many languages,
and his collections include *Collected Love Poems*,
Armada and, from Penguin, *Selected Poems*. His
verse for children includes *Gargling with Jelly*,
Gargling with Gerbils and *Thawing Frozen Frogs*.
Brian Patten is a popular performer of his work,
and he has also written children's plays as well as
editing *The Puffin Book of Modern Children's Verse* and
The Puffin Book of Utterly Brilliant Poetry.

www.brianpat

II0657207

Lancashire County Library

30118131960886

Books by Brian Patten

Poetry

GARGLING WITH JELLY

JUGGLING WITH GERBILS

THAWING FROZEN FROGS

THE UTTER NUTTERS

THE PUFFIN BOOK OF 20TH CENTURY
VERSE (Ed.)

THE PUFFIN BOOK OF UTTERLY
BRILLIANT POETRY (Ed.)

Picture Books

BEN'S MAGIC TELESCOPE

LITTLE HOTCHPOTCH

THE MAGIC BICYCLE

Fiction

IMPOSSIBLE PARENTS

IMPOSSIBLE PARENTS GO GREEN

GARGLING
with Jelly

BRIAN
PATTEN

Illustrated by Chris Riddell

PUFFIN POETRY

Lancashire Library Services	
30118131960886	
PETERS	J821PAT
£6.99	23-Nov-2015
EBU	

PUFFIN BOOKS

UK | USA | Canada | Ireland | Australia
India | New Zealand | South Africa

Puffin Books is part of the Penguin Random House group of companies
whose addresses can be found at global.penguinrandomhouse.com.

puffinbooks.com

Penguin
Random House
UK

First published in Viking Kestrel 1985
Published in Puffin Books 1986
Reissued in this edition 2015
001

Text copyright © Brian Patten, 1985
Illustrations copyright © Chris Riddell, 2003

The moral right of the author and illustrator has been asserted

Printed in Great Britain by Clays Ltd, St Ives plc

A CIP catalogue record for this book is available from the British Library

ISBN: 978-0-141-36295-3

www.greenpenguin.co.uk

MIX
Paper from
responsible sources
FSC
www.fsc.org   FSC® C018179

Penguin Random House is committed to a
sustainable future for our business, our readers
and our planet. This book is made from Forest
Stewardship Council® certified paper.

Contents

Squeezes

We love to squeeze bananas,
We love to squeeze ripe plums,
And when they are feeling sad
We love to squeeze our mums.

Mum Won't Let Me Keep a Rabbit

Mum won't let me keep a rabbit,
She won't let me keep a bat,
She won't let me keep a porcupine
Or a water-rat.

I can't keep pigeons
And I can't keep snails,
I can't keep kangaroos
Or wallabies with nails.

She won't let me keep a rattlesnake
Or viper in the house,
She won't let me keep a mamba
Or its meal, a mouse.

She won't let me keep a wombat
And it isn't very clear
Why I can't keep iguanas,
Jellyfish or deer.

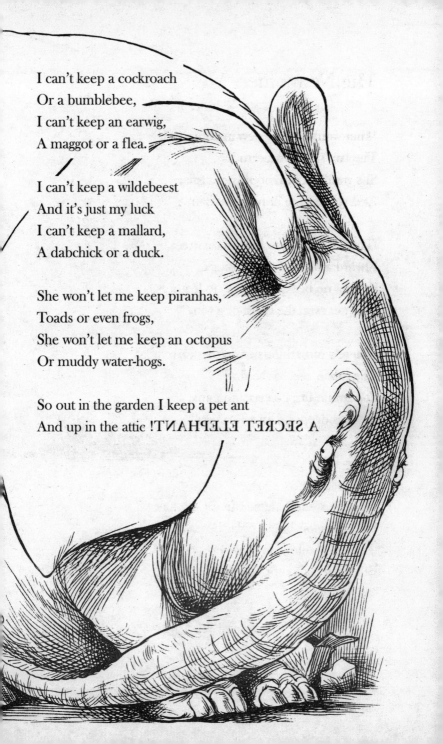

I can't keep a cockroach
Or a bumblebee,
I can't keep an earwig,
A maggot or a flea.

I can't keep a wildebeest
And it's just my luck
I can't keep a mallard,
A dabchick or a duck.

She won't let me keep piranhas,
Toads or even frogs,
She won't let me keep an octopus
Or muddy water-hogs.

So out in the garden I keep a pet ant
And up in the attic A SECRET ELEPHANT!

The Newcomer

'There's something new in the river,'
The fish said as it swam,
'It's got no scales, no fins, no gills,
And ignores the impassable dam.'

'There's something new in the trees,'
I heard a bloated thrush sing,
'It's got no beak, no claws, no feathers,
And not even the ghost of a wing.'

'There's something new in the warren,'
The rabbit said to the doe,
'It's got no fur, no eyes, no paws,
Yet digs deeper than we can go.'

'There's something new in the whiteness,'
Said the snow-bright polar bear,
'I saw its shadow on a glacier
But it left no footprints there.'

Throughout the animal kingdom
The news was spreading fast –

No beak no claws no feathers,
No scales no fur no gills,
It lives in the trees and the water,
In the earth and the snow and the hills,
And it kills and it kills and it kills.

Cousin Lesley's See-through Stomach

Cousin Lesley took a pill
That made her go invisible.
Perhaps this would have been all right
If everything was out of sight.

But all around her stomach swam
Half-digested bread and jam,
And no matter how she tried
She couldn't hide what was inside.

In the morning we often noted
How the toast and porridge floated,
And how unappetizing in the light
Was the curry from last night.

Some Gruyère had fallen victim
To her strange digestive system,
And there seemed a million ways
To digest old mayonnaise.

We were often fascinated
By the stuff left undigested,
A mish-mash of peas and jelly
Drifted round our cousin's belly.

Certain bits of Cornish pastie
Looked repugnant and quite nasty,
While the strawberries from last year
Were without the cream, I fear.

And at dinner, oh dear me!
What a disgusting sight to see
Chewed-up fish and cold brown tea
Where Cousin Lesley's tum should be.

Burying the Dog in the Garden

When we buried
the dog in
the garden on
the grave we put
a cross and
the tall man
next door was
cross.
'Animals have no
souls,' he said.
'They must have animal
souls,' we said. 'No,'
he said and
shook his head.
'Do you need a
soul to go
to Heaven?' we
asked. He nodded
his head. 'Yes,'
he said.
'That means my
hamster's not
in Heaven,' said

Kevin. 'Nor is
my dog,' I said.
'My cat could sneak
in anywhere,' said
Clare. And we thought
what a strange place Heaven
must be with
nothing to stroke
for eternity.
We were all
seven.
We decided we
did not want to
go to Heaven.
For that the
tall man next
door is to blame.

I've Never Heard the Queen Sneeze

I've never heard the Queen sneeze
Or seen her blow her nose,
I've never seen her pick a spot
Or tread on someone's toes,
I've never seen her slide upon
A slippery piece of ice,
I've never seen her frown and say
'This jelly is not nice!'
I've never seen her stick a finger
In her royal and waxy ear,
I've never seen her take it out
And sniff, and say 'Oh dear!'
I've never seen her swap her jewels
Or play frisbee with her crown,
I've never seen her spill her soup
Or drop porridge on her gown,
I wonder what she does
When she sits at home alone,
Playing with her corgies
And throwing them a bone?
I bet they've seen the Queen sneeze
And seen her blow her nose,
I bet they've seen her pick a spot
And tread on someone's toes.

I bet they've seen her slide upon
A slippery piece of ice,
I bet they've seen her frown and say,
'This jelly is not nice!'
I bet they've seen her stick a finger
In her royal and waxy ear,
I bet they've seen her take it out
And sniff, and say 'Oh dear!'
I bet they've seen her swap her jewels
And play frisbee with her crown,
I bet they've seen her spill her soup
And drop porridge on her gown.
So why can't I do all these things
Without being sent to bed?
Or failing that, why can't I
Be made the Queen instead?

The Witch's Pickle

Have you ever tried to tickle
A witch's pickle in the dark,
And tried to make it giggle
And scream: 'What a lark!'?
That's exactly what I did
So I think you'd better not
'Cause now I'm truly pickled
And in the witch's pot!

The Bee's Last Journey to the Rose

I came first through the warm grass
Humming with spring,
And now swim through the evening's
Soft sunlight gone cold.
I'm old in this green ocean,
Going a final time to the rose.

North Wind, until I reach it,
Keep your icy breath away
That changes pollen into dust.
Let me be drunk on this scent a final time.
Then blow if you must.

The Children's Fall-out Shelter

Deep in their underground shelter
Three people sit in the dark,
Remembering how when they were children
The world was lit by a spark.

They were placed in underground shelters
By parents who did not survive.
They were packed into underground shelters
Like bees packed into a hive.

Tom had wanted to be a farmer
But the earth was bare as a stone

Bill had wanted to be a hermit
But found no place to be alone

Susan had wanted to travel
But the earth was covered in flame

So they sat in their underground shelter
Wondering who was to blame.

Now deep in their underground shelter
Three old people sit in the dark,
Recalling stories of the fire-flood
And of the fire-proof Ark.

Deep in their underground shelter,
Safe from poison and from flames,
They shape coffins out of the cradles
Upon which were written their names.

Billy Dreamer's Fantastic Friends

The Incredible Hulk came to tea,
Robin was with him too,
Batman stayed at home that night
Because his bat had flu.

Superman called to say hello
And Spiderman spun us a joke.
Dynamite Sue was supposed to come
But she went up in smoke.

The Invisible Man might have called,
But as I wasn't sure,
I left an empty chair and bun
Beside the kitchen door.

They signed my autograph book,
But I dropped it in the fire.
Now whenever I tell my friends
They say I'm a terrible liar.

But incredible people *do* call round
('Specially when I'm alone),
And if they don't, and I get bored,
I call them on the phone.

Thin Soup

Sitting in a cold tureen
  The miser's soup
Looked clear and clean.
  There was neither
Spud nor bean;
  It was in fact
Quite without
  A single carrot
Or a sprout.
  It was unsullied
By salt or meat;
  It was neither
Sour nor sweet.
  Though it contained
Several bubbles
  It was free
Of any troubles.
  Cooking it
Took half a minute
  As there was really
Nothing in it.

The Lion and the Echo

The King of the Beasts, deep in the wood,
Roared as loudly as it could.
Right away the echo came back
And the lion thought itself under attack.

'What voice is it that roars like mine?'
The echo replied, 'Mine, mine.'

'Who might you be?' asked the furious lion,
'I'm king of this jungle, this jungle is mine.'
And the echo came back a second time,
'This jungle is mine, is mine, is mine.'

The lion swore revenge if only it could
Discover the intruder in the wood.
It roared, 'Coward! Come out and show yourself!'
But the fearless echo replied simply, '. . . elf.'

'Come out,' roared the lion, 'enough deceit,
Do you fear for your own defeat?'
But all the echo did was repeat,
'Defeat . . . defeat . . .'

Frightened by every conceivable sound,
The exhausted lion sank to the ground.
A bird in a tree looked down and it said,
'Dear lion, I'm afraid that what you hear
Is simply the voice of your lion-sized fear.'

The Bossy Young Tree

'Fallen leaves,' said the tree,
'Are merely debris.
Do ask the wind
To blow them away.'

'Before a year can pass
They will rot into me,
So don't be an ass,'
Said the grass.

'Bah!' said the tree,
'They are still debris,
So do ask the wind
To blow them away.'

'Don't be so vicious,
They are quite nutritious,
As you will soon see
When they rot into me.'

'They're keeping you warm,' said the tree,
'And you want them to stay
Because they're covering you
Like a double duvet.'

'They're keeping me damp,' said the grass,
'And I'm bound to get cramp
But I think they should stay
And rot the natural way.'

'I insist,' said the tree.
'I do not want debris
Littering the ground
In front of me.'

'It's ecologically sound
To have leaves on the ground.
With them you'll thrive,
But without won't survive.'

'Are you sure?' said the tree.
'Yes,' said the the grass.
'Then let it pass,' said the tree,
'I was being an ass.'

'Did you call?' said the wind.
'Oh no,' said the tree,
'I was merely admiring
This lovely debris.'

The Moggitiflew

The Moggitiflew was a marvellous thing –
Three eyes, two heads, a bit of a wing.
It lived in a tree in a park in the town,
It wore a string vest and an old dressing gown.
It was wise as an owl and white as a swan.
Once there were two but now there are none.

This is a shame and a bit of a pity,
The last was trampled to death in Manchester City.

Embryonic Mega-stars

We can play reggae music, funk and skiffle too,
We prefer heavy metal but the classics sometimes do.
We're keen on Tamla-Motown, folk and soul,
But most of all, what we like
Is basic rock and roll.
We can play the monochord, the heptachord and flute,
We're OK on the saxophone and think the glockenspiel is
    cute,
We really love the tuba, the balalaika and guitar
And our duets on the clavichord are bound to take us far.
We think castanets are smashing, harmonicas are fun,
And with the ocarina have only just begun.
We've mastered synthesizers, bassoons and violins
As well as hurdy-gurdies, pan pipes and mandolins.
The tom-tom and the tabor, the trumpet and the drum
We learnt to play in between the tintinnabulum.
We want to form a pop group
And will when we're eleven,
But at the moment Tracey's eight
And I am only seven.

Last of My Kind

Was a giant
Not long ago,
Sat in wood,
Watched things grow.

Was the last
Of his kind,
Sat in wood,
Did not mind

When the rain
Fell on head,
When the fox
Shared his bed.

Not long ago
Was a witch.
Happy thing
Lived in ditch.

Was the last
Of her kind,
Wore old rags,
Did not mind.

Giant and witch
Sometimes talked,
In the wood
Sometimes walked.

Doctor came
Took witch away,
In a home
Had to stay.

Had not meant
To be unkind.
Said poor witch
Was out of mind.

She spoke of giant,
Spoke of fern,
To the ditch
Wished to return.

Pined and sighed,
Sad to say,
In a month
Passed away.

Though giant kept
Out of sight
He tended ditch
Day and night.

He lived a year,
Lived a day,
Then giant too
Pined away.

All this happened
I might say
Mile or so
From motorway.

In the forest
I sometimes walk,
With giant's ghost
Sometimes talk.

He tells me all
This is true,
Now I'm telling
Back to you.

I believe,
For you see,
I believe
Witch ordinary.

And the giant,
That he too
Was human as
You and you.

Giant was simple
As a babe,
Witch's mind
Like a cave,

And both lived
A different way
To what's expected
Now today.

I too live
In the wood,
Live on leaves
And rabbits' blood.

Munch the leaves,
Read the stars,
From hidey-hole
Watch the cars.

Am the last
Of my kind,
Do not wish
To be defined.

Why I Haven't Got a Smollypopomouse

I haven't got a Smurgle or a Zurgle in the house,
I haven't even got a Smollypopomouse.
So I went to the pet shop and said, 'What I want
Is a Smurgle or a Zurgle
Or a Smollypopomouse.'
The man behind the counter smiled and shook his head.
'You'll have to go to Venus for one of them,' he said.
So I went to the travel shop and said, 'What I want
Is a ticket to go and get a Smollypopomouse.'
He had tickets for Africa and tickets for Peru
But I frowned and said none of them would do.
So I went up the road and had a word with the vet.
He said Smollypopomouses were impossible to get.
So I went down the road and I went to the zoo.
I looked around for ages and there were none there too.
So I went and asked Mum, who said, 'I'll have to think.'
And she asked Dad, who didn't even blink.
They both asked if I'd like another kind of pet
As Smollypopomouses seemed rather hard to get.
That's why I've got a hamster and a kitten in the house,
But haven't got a Smurgle or a Zurgle
Or a Smollypopomouse.

Tommy Tosh and Susie Leek

When Susie Leek meets Tommy Tosh
Behind a bush they blush.
When Tommy Tosh meets Susie Leek
He finds it really hard to speak
Or say exactly why they rush
Behind that bush to blush.

Five Nasty Goblins

All goblins are nasty and the nastiest of all
Received this invitation to Hobgoblin Hall:

There is a ball in the Hall
at half past nine.
Please come along to
sup and dine
SIGNED: The Hobgoblin
RSVP

The first to go was very sly.
He picked his nose and wondered why
The Hobgoblin had invited them all
To the mysterious Hobgoblin Hall.

The second thought he'd take a swan,
So brained one with a frying pan.

The third went to the ball on a log
Hauled along by a friendly frog.

The fourth rode by on a rat called Tomb
And sneered at anything likely to bloom.

The fifth cut hedgerows to resemble
Things that made the others tremble.

They saw a sign saying, 'This way to the ball',
Then saw in the distance – Hobgoblin Hall!

A butler-ghost said, 'The ball's begun.
Do come in and have some fun.'

The goblin who was very sly
Still picked his nose and wondered why
The Hobgoblin had invited them all
To the mysterious Hobgoblin Hall.

The second goblin ate swan pie all night
And was sick on everyone in sight.

The third goblin and his friend the frog
Got roaring drunk on Goblin Grog.

The Hobgoblin's peculiar cat
Ate the fourth goblin's rat.

The fifth goblin got into a terrible fight
Because he had given the others a fright.

At midnight when they could take no more
And found five locks on the ballroom door
They realized the Hobgoblin had arranged the ball
To prove that *he* was the worst of all!
They screamed and howled and went blue in the face
But nobody ever came near that place.
They stayed till the signs rotted out on the moor
And the five locks crumbled from the ballroom door.
Then the five nasty goblins hurried home through the rain
And smiled when they said they'd not be nasty again.

Tall Story

The sole survivor of an atomic war
(Who was also a bit of a joker)
Arrived in a land where everything
Had forgotten what it was.

He said to an old tree
'Repeat after me, "I am a bomb."'
'I am a bomb,' said the old tree,
And promptly exploded.

This goes to show
You can never be too careful if
You are
The sole survivor.

Gust Becos I Cud Not Spel

Gust becos I cud not spel
It did not mean I was daft
When the boys in school red my riting
Some of them laffed

But now I am the dictater
They have to rite like me
Utherwise they cannot pas
The GCSE

Some of the girls wer ok
But those who laffed a lot
Have al bean rownded up
And hav recintly bean shot

The teecher who corrected my speling
As not been shot at al
But four the last fifteen howers
As bean standing up against a wal

He has to stand ther until he can spel
Figgymisgrugifooniyn the rite way
I think he will stand ther forever
I just inventid it today

The Bone

The blind king sat alone
On his magic throne
And was thrown
To feel a bone
Fall on his gown.
(It made him frown.)
Somewhere in town
The man who'd thrown
The well-gnawed bone
Was heard to moan.
'Because no seed's grown
I gnawed the bone
That was thrown.'

'If no seed had grown
Then this bone
Fallen on your gown
Is all we own,'
Said the magic throne.
The blind king agreed
And he decreed
More seed be sown
And the bone
Be placed alone
In a case in case
The rich should moan
They hadn't a bone.

The Trouble with My Sister

My little sister was truly awful,
She was really shocking,
She put the budgie in the fridge
And slugs in Mummy's stocking.

She was really awful,
But it was a load of fun
When she stole old Uncle Wilbur's
Double-barrelled gun.

She aimed it at a pork pie
And blew it into bits,
She aimed it at a hamster
That was having fits.

She leapt up on the telly,
She pirouetted on the cat,
She gargled with some jelly
And spat in Grandad's hat.

She ran down the hallway,
She ran across the road,
She dug up lots of little worms
And caught a squirming toad.

She put them in a large pot
And she began to stir,
She added a pint of bat's blood
And some rabbit fur.

She leapt upon the Hoover,
Around the room she went.
Once she had a turned-up nose
But now her nose is bent.

I like my little sister,
There is really just one hitch,
I think my little sister
Has become a little witch.

The Trouble with My Brother

Thomas was only three
And though he was not fat
We knew that there was something wrong
When he ate the cat.

Nibble, nibble, munch, munch,
Nibble, nibble, munch,
Nibble, nibble, munch, munch,
He had the cat for lunch!

He ate a lump of coal,
He ate a candlestick
And when he ate the tortoise
Mother felt quite sick.

Nibble, nibble, munch, munch,
Nibble, nibble, munch,
Nibble, nibble, munch, munch,
A tortoise for lunch!

When he was a boy of four
He went to the zoo by bus
And alarmed us all by eating
A hippopotamus.

Nibble, nibble, munch, munch,
Nibble, nibble, munch,
Nibble, nibble, munch, munch,
A hippopotamus for lunch!

When he went to school
We tried to warn the teacher
But Thomas pounced long before
Anyone could reach her.

Nibble, nibble, munch, munch,
Nibble, nibble, munch,
Nibble, nibble, munch, munch,
A teacher for lunch!

We used to get nice letters
So Mum was full of grief
When upon the doorstep
She found the postman's teeth.

Nibble, nibble, munch, munch,
Nibble, nibble, munch,
Nibble, nibble, munch, munch,
A postman for lunch!

He ate thirteen baby-sitters
(We often heard their squeals)
He ate a social worker
In between these meals.

Nibble, nibble, munch, munch,
Nibble, nibble, munch,
Nibble, nibble, munch, munch,
A social worker for lunch!

A policeman came to have a word
About what was going on,
Thomas took a shine to him
And soon he was all gone.

Nibble, nibble, munch, munch,
Nibble, nibble, munch,
Nibble, nibble, munch, munch,
A policeman for lunch!

None of us says much,
It holds us all in thrall,
Having a little brother
Who is a cannibal.

Nibble, nibble, munch, munch,
Nibble, nibble, munch,
At supper time we hide away,
Nibble, nibble, munch!

The Apple-flavoured Worm

When the rivers were pregnant with fishes
And the trees were pregnant with buds,
When the earth was fat with seeds
And a million other goods,
Taking a snooze in an apple
Was an apple-flavoured worm.
It heard God's voice say, 'Bite.
Eve, it is your turn.'

When the sky was bluer than blue
And the earth shone bright as a pin,
Before Paradise had been abandoned
Or a tongue had invented a sin,
Taking a snooze in an apple
Was the apple-flavoured worm.
It heard God's voice say, 'Bite.
Adam, it's now your turn.'

Then the bloom was gone from the garden,
The first petal had dropped from a flower,
The wound in the rib's cage was healed
And Satan had lived for an hour.
And wide awake in the apple
The apple-flavoured worm
Heard the Gates of Heaven closing
And a key of iron turn.

The Plague and the Fox

There was a plague among the chickens,
There was a plague among the rats,
There was a plague among the ravens
and the mice and voles and bats.

There was a plague among the rabbits,
There was a plague among the hogs,
There was a plague among the salmon
and among the toads and frogs.

There was a plague among the squirrels,
There was a plague among the cats,
There was a plague among the herons
and the fish and water-rats.

There was a plague among the weasels,
There was a plague among the cows,
There was a plague among the badgers
and the stoats and owls and sows.

There was a plague among the pigeons,
There was a plague among the snails,
There was a plague among the sparrows
and the sheep and geese and quails.

There was a fox who knew the cure.
They went knocking on his door.
Only the fox knew the cure.

'Dr Fox, please come and treat us
For once we are all agreed
You must do your best to cure us
If you want your food unplagued.'

But Dr Fox did not answer.
From his den came no reply.
He'd scarpered from the stricken wood
and left the food to die.

Looking for Dad

Whenever Mum and Dad
were full of gloom
they always yelled,
'*Tidy up your room!*'
Just because my comics were
scattered here and
everywhere and
because I did not care
where I left my underwear
they yelled,
'*You can't watch TV today*
if you don't tidy
all those things away!'
Then one day they
could not care less
about the room's
awful mess.
They seemed more intent
on a domestic argument.
They both looked glum
and instead of me Dad
screeched at Mum.

One night when I
went to bed he
simply vanished.
I had not tidied
up my room because
I too was full of gloom.
That night I dreamt
Dad was hidden
beneath the things
I'd been given.
In my dream
I was in despair
and flung about
my underwear
but could not find
him anywhere.
I looked for him
lots and lots
beneath crumpled sheets
and old robots.
I looked in cupboards
and in shoes.
I looked up all
the chimney flues.
I remembered how
he'd seemed to be
unhappier than

49

even me. When I woke I knew
it was not my room
that filled Mum and Dad
with so much gloom.
Now I stare at all
my old toy cars
and carpets stained
with old Mars bars
and hope he will
come back soon
and admire my very tidy room.

Never Shake a Baby

Because Henry went on crying
And kept us all awake,
I took him from his little cot
And gave him a good shake.

Henry would not stop then
It was plain for all to see
Henry would go on crying
In the pitch of middle C.

Soon the room began to fill
With Henry's salty tears,
He screeched and bawled and burbled
And realized our worst fears.

Soon the chairs were floating,
The cat got more than wet,
We put it in a plastic bag
And sent it to the vet.

While Granny doggie-paddled
And blocked up both her ears
Henry drowned the goldfish
With his salty tears.

They spilt into the roadway,
They stopped the motor cars,
The drivers screeched and shouted
At that kid of ours.

Henry floated through the window
Upon a wooden chair,
Mother threw her hands up
And shouted in despair:

'Henry, stop your crying!
Henry, dear, you must!
Henry, stop your crying
Or we'll all be drowned and lost!'

We got some expert jugglers
And the world's most famous clown,
We even got a hypnotist
To try and calm him down,

But Henry went on crying
And soon from East to West
Everyone was swimming
And saying, 'What a pest!'

'Henry, stop your crying!
Henry, dear, you must!
Henry, stop your crying
Or we'll all be drowned, or rust!'

Henry did not hear them,
On and on he went,
Businesses went bankrupt,
He brought down the government.

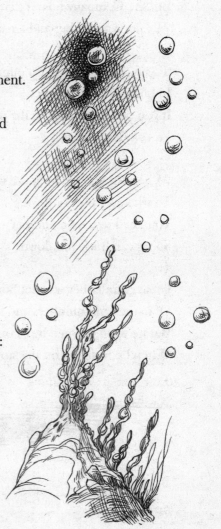

Now most of Britain's vanished
Beneath a sea of tears,
People sail right over it
And will for many years.

And sitting on a mountain top
Mum's still in despair,
And Henry is still floating
Upon his wooden chair.

So please listen to my warning:
Even if you're kept awake
Never take a baby from its cot
And give it a good shake.

Running Away

My great-grandfather ran away to sea,
My father would have done the same,
But the Company bosses said to him,
'We need a number and a name.

'If you don't show up on our computer
In black or white or grey,
If you don't show up on the computer
You cannot run away.

'Wherever you sail to in the world,
To whatever port or town,
You need to have a number
So we can track you down.'

Great-grandfather was not born free
Of names and numbers and forms,
But he wasn't owned by a computer
When he rode out on the storms.

And now that I have come of age
And it's two thousand and eighty-three
I want to run away to space
But the Company bosses say to me:

'If you don't show up on the computer
In black or white or grey,
If you don't show up on the computer
You cannot run away.'

What the Headless Ghost's Head Wants Most of All

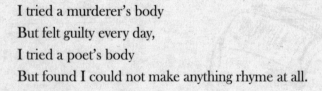

I tried a sailor's body
But was seasick all the time,
I tried a policeman's body
But then indulged in crime.

I tried a cowboy's body
But could not shoot a gun,
I tried a teacher's body
But it wasn't any fun.

I tried a murderer's body
But felt guilty every day,
I tried a poet's body
But found I could not make anything rhyme at all.

I tried a judge's body
But the wig did not fit,
I tried a boxer's body
But all I got was hit.

I want my own body back!
Even in a sack!
Even if the bones are broken
I want my own body back!

I tried a pop-star's body
But I found I could not sing,
I tried a Scotsman's body
But could not do the fling.

I tried a dustman's body
But could not stand the smell.
I tried an angel's body
But ended up in Hell.

I want my own body back!
Even in a sack!
Even if the bones are broken
I want my own body back!

Neddy Norris and the Useless Anteater

It was two days after the picnic
On which Neddy tortured the ants
That the ghost of the first one haunted him
By climbing up his pants.

The next day a second ant
Bit him on the toe,
The day after this another
Decided to have a go.

There must have been six thousand ants
And the ghost of each one swore
It would nibble Neddy Norris
Till Neddy Norris was no more.

Neddy went into a pet shop
And he bought a tame anteater.
He thought with glee: 'Now I'll be safe,
And life will be much sweeter.'

The anteater was rather placid –
Though it saw what was going on
It stared at the ants as they marched past
Without eating a single one.

Neddy continued to be bitten,
He howled and made a din.
His family grew fed up
And threw him in the bin.

Now the ghostly voice of Neddy Norris
Moans at the failure of his plan,
For he never guessed the anteater
Was a vegetarian.

Pals

I'm sorry for shouting,
Let's be pals.
I was wrong the other day.
All those months of being friends I've startled away,
Like a flock of frightened birds.

Guess What Dad Does

When I went to junior school
My friends asked what Dad did,
I did not dare to tell them,
So I had to ad lib.

My father's not a fireman.
He's not a bus conductor.
He's not a stuntman in the films
Or a PE instructor.

Yes, he is quite rich,
And no, he's not a banker.
He doesn't own a goldmine
Or an oil tanker.

I help him with his job,
And stay up late at night.
Dad works in the shadows
And does not like the light.

I like his job best of all
And get quite excited
When we enter people's homes
Totally uninvited.

I Saw a Thief

I saw a thief
　　steal my TV
and take it to his flat.
　　He stole the cups,
he stole the plates,
　　he stole the welcome mat.

He stole the bed,
　　he stole the chair,
and when he came back later,
　　he stole the mirror
and the desk
　　and refrigerator.

He went out to a café
　　and while he fed his face
I used a bunch of skeleton keys
　　and stole into his place.
When the thief got back home
　　and found me in the bed
he was annoyed and turned
　　a criminal shade of red.

I said do not worry,
    I sleep quiet as a mouse,
and anyway hadn't he
    just moved me to this house?

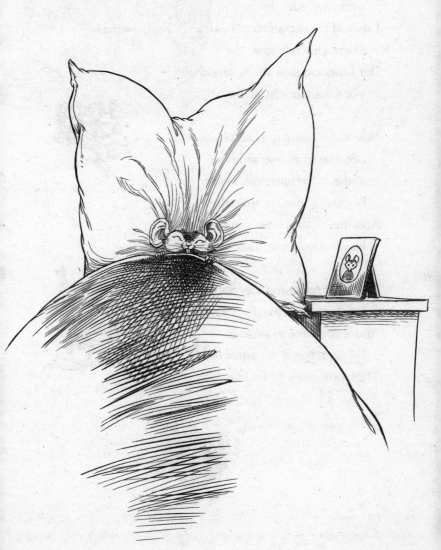

Someone Stole the

While I was taking a short   -nap
  someone stole the   ,
I should have spun round like a   herine wheel
  when someone stole the   .
But I was too slow to   ch them,
  when someone stole the   .

Now the   amaran can't float,
  because someone stole the   .
And the   erpillar can't crawl,
  because someone stole the   .
And the   aract can't fall,
  because someone stole the   .

It was not me and it was not you
  but it is   egorically true,
And if you were to ask me
  I'd say it was a   astrophe
That someone's stolen the   .

What Am I?

1.

I go to where I come from,
I'm always passing and I stay,
Though I never move an inch
I go many miles each day.

2.

People say I never existed
And that is the way it looks;
I'm only seen on inn-signs
And in picture books.

3.

I rust the locks from gate posts,
I never age but age,
I can be detected in a fossil
And upon a yellow page.

4.

Oil is something I like to sip,
Coal is something I like to guzzle,
I fried a knight the other day,
And now I wear a muzzle.

1. A road; 2. A unicorn; 3. Time; 4. A pet dragon!

Teacher's Pet

In our class the teacher's pet
Really is quite funny.
Yesterday he grew a tail
And now looks like a bunny.

The Venus Take-away

When me and my robot blast off to play
We stop at the Venus Take-away.
I have Jamaican patties and he
Has a micro-chip buttie.

Rules

Governments rule most countries,
Bankers rule most banks,
Captains rule their football teams
And piranhas rule fish tanks.

There are rules for gnobling gnomes
And rules for frying frogs,
There are rules for biting bullies
And for vexing vicious dogs.

There are rules for driving motor cars
And crashing into chums,
There are rules for taking off your pants
And showing spotty bums.

There are rules for nasty children
Who tie bangers to old cats,
There are rules for running riot
And rules for burning bats.

There are rules in the classroom.
There are rules in the street.
Some rules are wild and woolly
And some are tame and neat.

And some are pretty sensible
And some are pretty daft;
Some I take quite seriously,
At others I have laughed,

But there is one special rule
You should not be without:
If you do not like the rules
OPEN YOUR MOUTH AND SHOUT!
OPEN YOUR MOUTH AND SHOUT!

The School Caretaker

In the corner of the playground
Down dark and slimy stairs,
Lived a monster with a big nose
Full of curly hairs.

He had a bunch of keyrings
Carved out of little boys,
He confiscated comics
And all our favourite toys.

He wore a greasy uniform,
Looked like an undertaker,
More scary than a horror film,
He was the school caretaker.

I left the school some years ago;
Saw him again the other day.
He looked rather sad and old
Shuffling on his way.

It's funny when you grow up
How grown-ups start growing down,
And the snarls upon their faces
Are no more than a frown.

In the corner of the playground
Down dark and slimy stairs,
Sits a lonely little man
With a nose full of curly hairs.

Happy Jalopy

The motor car is broken
 and now it can't be driven
it's become a house
 for the tramp to live in.
His bedroom's in the back seat
 and he doesn't make a fuss
when the wind and rain blow
 through the broken glass.
He says it's very spacious
 and he's very happy
living with his cat
 in the old jalopy.

The Terrible Path

While playing at the woodland's edge
I saw a child one day,
She was standing near a foaming brook
And a sign half rotted away.

There was something strange about her clothes;
They were from another age,
I might have seen them in a book
Upon a mildewed page.

She looked pale and frightened,
Her voice was thick with dread.
She spoke through lips rimmed with green
And this is what she said:

'*I saw a signpost with no name,*
I was surprised and had to stare,
It pointed to a broken gate
And a path that led nowhere.

'*The path had run to seed and I*
Walked as in a dream.
It entered a silent oak wood,
And crossed a silent stream.

'And in a tree a silent bird
Mouthed a silent song.
I wanted to turn back again
But something had gone wrong.

'The path would not let me go;
It had claimed me for its own,
It led me through a dark wood
Where all was overgrown.

'I followed it until the leaves
Had fallen from the trees,
I followed it until the frost
Drugged the autumn's bees.

'I followed it until the spring
Dissolved the winter snow,
And whichever way it turned
I was obliged to go.

'The years passed like shooting stars,
They melted and were gone,
But the path itself seemed endless,
It twisted and went on.

'*I followed it and thought aloud,*
"*I'll be found, wait and see.*"
Yet in my heart I knew by then
The world had forgotten me.'

Frightened I turned homeward,
But stopped and had to stare.
I too saw that signpost with no name,
And the path that led nowhere.

The Vicar and the Fleas

Mrs Mullion's lonely
Now the vicar does not call,
He says he itched far too much
And won't go there at all.
For Mrs Mullion had a thousand
Cats with a zillion fleas,
And though he no longer visits
She's not all that displeased,
For she knows each cat's a million times
More meek and mild than he,
And that God himself would not mind
Being bitten by a flea.

The Complaint

'It will not last!'

'Who said that?' demanded the dragonfly,
Morning-blown, oblivious of sorrow.

'The best has passed!'

'Who blasphemed just then?'
Inquired the wren.

'All perishes!'

'How absurd!' said the gnat,
'What idiot believes that?'

All listened for an answer.
None came.

Night fell on Paradise,
Its children slept.
Hunched outside the Gates Adam wept.

The Saga of the Doomed Cyclist

When Harry Harris knocked a witch
Into a muddy roadside ditch
She put a spell upon his bike:
'Ride forever, little tike!'
Harry thought it might be fun, but hardly
   had the boy begun
To ride his bike to Timbuktu
Than a hill came into view.
He puffed and panted, reached the top,
But even then he could not stop.
He cycled right past Leamington Spa on his way to
   Shangri-La.
He knocked a copper down for six, shouting,
'You really should arrest that witch!
It is her fault I cannot stop, all I want to do is flop.
My back is aching, my legs are dead,
I want to crawl back home to bed.'
He cycled all the way to Dover.
He went under the Channel and then over
Every mountain in the Pyrenees
Where frost and sunlight burnt his knees.
He cycled across the plains of Spain,
He was attacked by bulls and drenched in rain.
Cycling under the Mediterranean

He acquired a peculiar aqua-tan.
Right through Africa he went, crashing into a Bedouin's
    tent.
Snakes and lions galore he saw,
He'd never cycled so fast before.
When Mount Kilimanjaro came into view
He wondered what on earth to do.
He swung up through Egypt and the Nile
And cycled over a crocodile.
On and on and on he went –
He found no way to turn back
And soon had cycled through Iraq.
The witch was a lady he'd begun to hate
As he cycled parched through parched Kuwait.
He quickly made it through Iran
Into the mountains of Afghanistan.
And he was tired as a boy could be
By the time he reached Dushanbe.
He rode through Russia where the biggest hurdle
Was navigating the Arctic Circle.
His wheels were frozen, it took several nights
To slide across the Bering Straits.
He thought: 'If I meet that witch I'll ask her
If I can stop before Alaska.'
But as she was nowhere to be seen
He kept on pushing that machine.
Pedalling madly through the Yukon

He wished he'd something warmer on,
And halfway through Ontario
He was up to his neck in frozen snow.
He thought he was lost, his bike was a wreck
By the time he made it through Quebec.
In Newfoundland he had a notion
He'd crash headlong into the ocean,
But instead he cycled up an old gangplank
On to a fishing boat that stank.
For three storm-tossed weeks round the deck he went,
His wheels were buckled, his frame was bent.
Flying-fish and seagulls made salty jokes,
Waves left seaweed in his spokes.
The poor boy was seasick day and night,
His face turned green and then turned white.

He arrived in Liverpool Docks and sighed:
'Never again will I knock a witch
Into a muddy roadside ditch.'
                    B U T ! ! !
Getting off the bike he found
His feet just wouldn't touch the ground.
He remembered the curse on him and his bike:
'Ride *forever*, little tike!'
As there seemed nowhere he could stay,
He cycle-navigated the world another way.
So no matter if you're in Leamington Spa

Or in exotic Shangri-La,
No matter if you're in oil-rich Arabia
Or staying with an aunt in Belgravia,
No matter if you're sucking soda-pop in Austin
Or trekking through the Glacial Basin,
Even if you're rescuing leprechauns from the Liffey
Or sailing on a raft down the Mississippi,
Even if you're picking flowers for your mum in Kew
Or on Bikini Atoll with nothing to do,
It's possible you'll see an old man on a bike
And it's possible that old man might be
The boy who many years ago
Knocked a witch
Into a muddy roadside ditch.

It might be fun to look up the places Harry cycled through and trace his journey with an atlas, but watch out, there is one place mentioned in the poem that doesn't exist on any map.

I Don't Believe in Human-tales

I don't believe there's such a thing
As nasty little boys.
I think that someone dreams them up;
It's one of the gnome-ups' ploys.

I don't believe in super-stores
Where bits of wings and legs
Of harmless little chickens
Are sold in plastic bags.

I'm sure it is just rubbish
That we get turned to stone
If we go near garden ponds
When we're playing out alone.

I'm sure gnome-ups invent these things
To scare us little gnomes
So we'll never leave the forests
Under which we have our homes.

The Whale's Hymn

In an ocean before cold dawn broke
Covered by an overcoat
I lay awake in a boat
And heard a whale.

Hearing a song so solemn and so calm
It seemed absurd to feel alarm –
But I had a notion it sang
God's favourite hymn,

And spoke direct to Him.

Winifred Weasel

Miss Winifred Weasel long and thin
All night sneaked around the farm,
Until she came to a narrow gap,
Newly opened in the barn.

Winifred Weasel long and thin
Squeezed her frame neatly in!

Miss Winifred Weasel felt at ease.
She was quite amazed at all she saw:
She attacked the carrots and the cheese,
And kept one eye upon the door.

Winifred Weasel long and thin
Squeezed her frame neatly in!

Miss Winifred Weasel nibbled and gnawed.
Rotund, then fat soon she grew,
And when the mouse came it deplored
How she had eaten enough for two.

Winifred Weasel long and thin
Squeezed her frame neatly in!

Suddenly outside the barn
She heard the noise of human feet.
She danced about in great alarm
But could find no way to retreat.

Winifred Weasel long and thin
Squeezed her frame neatly in!

She found the place where she got in,
But now the barn had become a trap.
She wished on her life she was still thin
And could squeeze out through that narrow gap.

Winifred Weasel once long and thin
Doomed by greed to be caged in!

The Jealous Mermaid

A mermaid in the ocean
Because she could not go ashore
Decided holidaymakers
Were really quite a bore.
She wanted them to go away
And finally got her wish
When from her underwater kitchen
She served up jellyfish.

The Little Ghost's Song

I'd like to be human again.
I'd like to get wet in the rain.
I wouldn't mind toothache
Just for living's sake!
I'd like to get wet in the rain.
I'd like to be human again.
I'd like to kick a ball
And my foot not go through at all!
What's the good of being a ghost
If you can't eat jam and toast?
If you can't pull a funny face,
Or be sent to bed in disgrace?
I'd rather be scared than scare,
I'd like to breathe some air.
I'd like to get wet in the rain.
I'd love to be human again!

Eight Brand New Angels
A Counting Rhyme

Ten creepy criminals trying to commit a crime.
One got caught and then there were nine.

Nine juicy children on a giant's dinner plate.
One got eaten up and then there were eight.

Eight brand new angels on their way to Heaven.
One fell back to earth and then there were seven.

Seven dare-devils crossing the River Styx.
One dived in and then there were six.

Six melancholic milliners admiring a beehive.
One put it on her head and then there were five.

Five young sons going off to war.
One got blown to bits and then there were four.

Four mischievous boys teasing a chimpanzee.
One teased a rattlesnake and then there were three.

Three trapeze artistes learning something new.
One failed to grasp the bar and then there were two.

Two men called Icarus flying towards the sun.
One quickly melted and then there was one.

One counting rhyme going on and on and on.
Suddenly it ended.
And then there was none.

The Pensive Pencils

I'm not scared of ghosts or of rats
Or of creaking doors or mice or bats,
I'm not scared of shadows or of owls
Or of hoots or squeaks or terrible growls,
I'm not scared of noises in the hall
Or of the things that slither and creep and crawl.
I'm not scared of things that moan and groan,
And I don't mind being left on my own,
But it's nearly midnight and I fear
The things I'm scared of are quite near.
It's horrible! It's terrible! I might seem a fool,
But I really can't stand being locked in school
B
    E
        C
           A
              U
                S
                  E

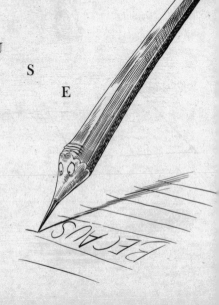

The Roundheads have come out of the history books,

There's a battle in the school hall,

There's a storm brewing up in the swimming-pool,

In fact it's become quite a squall.

The exercise books are puffing and panting,

They're doing press-ups in the gym,

The cat from the playground has joined them

In a feeble attempt to get slim.

There's a ghost of a cane in the cupboard,

The ex-pupils are rattling their bones,

The pens and the pencils are pensive,

And I'm locked in the school on my own!

The Computer Maniac and the Software Salesman

I tried to write a program
That suited birds and bees,
That would do away with office blocks
And make room for shrubs and trees,

So I studied other programs,
I punched away for hours.
I wrote programs for the rabbits
And programs for the flowers.

A man from Komputer Inc.
Came up to me and said:
'It's time that you integrated
Our software in your head.'

I was fed up with the Supersonic Mazes,
With In-Darth-Vaders from Outer Space,
I wanted to invent my own games
And be left in peace.

I hated how he controlled the hardware,
The spam-mail and magazines,
How he controlled all our games
And half our micro-dreams.

Other computer whizz-kids
Agreed with me as well.
They didn't like his software
They hated his hard-cell.

The man from Komputer Inc.
Tried to get away,
So we wired up his brain
And then began to play.

We played Pitfall and played Combat,
We played Froggers from Out-of-Space.
We played Bomb the Software Salesman,
And gave that creep no peace.

The man from Komputer Inc.
Shouted out for hours:
'For God's sake change the program,
Feed in the one you use for flowers!'

Groan-ups

When Jimmy Give-It-Us
And Sarah No-I-Won't-It's-Mine
Grew to be grown-ups
They were lonely all the time.
Their friends could not stand them
For all they did was whine
'Give-it-us-give-it-us-no-I-won't-it's-mine.'

There Was Once a Whole World in the Scarecrow

The farmer has dismantled the old scarecrow.
He has pulled out the straw and scattered it.
The wind has blown it away.
(A mouse once lived in its straw heart.)
He has taken off the old coat.
(In the torn pocket a grasshopper lived.)
He has thrown away the old shoes.
(In the left shoe a spider sheltered.)
He has taken away the hat.
(A little sparrow once nested there.)
And now the field is empty.
The little mouse has gone.
The grasshopper has gone.
The spider has gone.
The bird has gone.
The scarecrow,
Their world,
Has gone.
It has all gone.

The Complacent Tortoise

Languid, lethargic, listless and slow,
The tortoise would dally, an image of sloth.
'Immobile!' 'Complacent!' To the hare it was both.

'Enough of your insults, I seek satisfaction.
I'll run you a race and win by a fraction.'
Thus challenged the tortoise one afternoon.
'Right,' said the hare, 'let it be soon.'

They decided they'd race right through the wood
And the tortoise set off as fast as it could.
The hare followed at a leisurely pace
Quite confident it could win the race.

The tortoise thought as it ambled along,
'I have never been faster, or quite so strong.'
The hare on the other hand was often inclined
To stop at the roadside and improve its mind.

It read a fable by Aesop deep in the wood
Then of course it set off as fast as it could.
It decided it would put that fable aright
As it sped along with the speed of a light.

Languid, lethargic, listless and slow
The tortoise ran fast as a tortoise could go.
Yet the hare, having decided on saving face,
Quite easily managed to win the race.

'I feel,' said the tortoise, 'that I've been deceived,
For fables are things I've always believed.
I would love to have won a race so clearly designed
To point out a moral both old and refined.'

'Losing a race would not matter,' the hare said,
'For in speed Mother Nature placed me ahead.
Some fables are things you ought to contest –
Dear tortoise, in mine, I'm afraid you've come last.'

Snodding

When I broke a window
And my father said,
'Are you sure you didn't do it?'
I just snodded my head.
'Are you with us or against us?'
The school bully asked.
I snodded my head
Until the danger passed.
When I tell a lie
I turn bright red,
But I feel much safer
If I only snod my head.

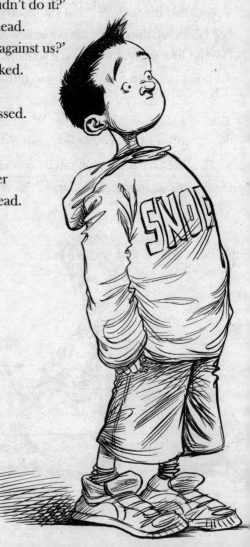

Please Explain

Have you ever tried explaining
A sundial to a bat,
Or taught a muddy little brother
The usage of a mat?
Have you ever tried explaining
A desert to a fish,
Or found a single wishing-well
In which you didn't want to wish?
If you have succeeded
Then please explain to me
Why it's always sunny at school-time
And rainy after tea.

Old Willy Wobbler

Willy Wobbler
  Shilly-shallied,
He wavered and
  He dawdled,
He dithered and
  He hummed and hawed
And stayed
  Undetermined.
When he was 103
  Death came along
And said:
  'Willy Wobbler,
Come and share
  My cold and
Final bed.'
  But Willy Wobbler
Shilly-shallied,
  He wavered and
He dawdled,
  He dithered and
He hummed and hawed
  And still
Stayed undetermined.

The PE Teacher Wants to Be Tarzan

The PE teacher sits and dreams
Of swinging through the trees,
Of taking jungle holidays
And crushing pythons with his knees,

Of running off with nice Miss Jones
The new biology teacher,
Of taking her to a posh tree-house
Where no one else can reach her.

Instead he puffs and pants all day
In a drab and dreary gym,
And wishes that there were a spell
For liberating him.

Double Glazing

Jenny lives in a flat on the nineteenth floor
Of South McDougle Street.
Through the smudged-up double-glazed windows
The world looks calm and neat.

Jenny does not complain much
About the giant holes in her shoes,
She prefers to stare out the window
And admire the distant views.

She'll not say nothing will Jenny,
About her pain and despair,
She's only a kid after all
And kids aren't supposed to care.

She'll not say nothing will Jenny,
She's a real tough nut to crack:
The kind of girl who always
Answers the teacher back.

Jenny lives in a flat on the nineteenth floor
Of South McDougle Street,
Through the smudged-up double-glazed windows
The world looks small and neat,

But down below it's crooked,
It is poor and full of hate,
And there are no double-glazed windows to stare through
When she's out and about the estate.

I Don't Want to Swap
My Model Racing Car

'What will you swap for your model racing car?'
'I don't want to swap my model racing car.'

'I'll swap a tin soldier or a spider's paw.'
'I don't want a tin soldier, I've had one before.'

'I'll swap a ticket to Canada or a pig's egg.'
'I've already got a ticket to go to Winnipeg.'

'I'll swap a pet snake or an elephant's wing.'
'I don't want a pet snake, I'm afraid it might sting.'

'I'll swap a pair of water-wings or a rabbit's beak.'
'I don't want a pair of water-wings, they would only leak.'

'How about a cage-bird or some grass-snake's hair?'
'Putting birds into cages isn't very fair.'

'What will you swap for that mangy old car?'
'I don't want to swap my model racing car.'

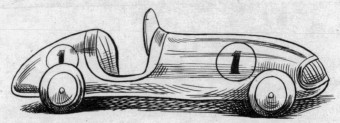

The Silly Siposark

'It is not going to rain
    so I won't come in the Ark.
The other animals are being daft,'
    said the silly Siposark.

The Friendless Moth

A moth with a long and Latin name
One day flew into a flame,
But because its problems were not shared
No one minded much or cared.
There was no one on whom it could depend,
It had no family or best friend.
I buried it one autumn dawn
Beneath a leaf out on the lawn.
I hope to Heaven it will ascend
And up there find a decent friend.

'Orange' Is a Lovely Word

'Orange' is a lovely word
    for which there is no rhyme,
it's such a fragrant scented special word
    it really is a crime
when dribbly drabbly little words
    such as 'bore' and 'sore'
have no trouble rhyming
    with words like 'Arkansas'.

The Toad and the Mayfly

Unearthing marble for a fountain
An archaeologist once found
Something unique and fabulous
Buried in the ground.

A toad, uncommon in appearance,
Crawled from under a stone.
It was annoyed at being woken
And said, 'I wish to be alone.

'I am quite separate from my species,
I am a toad apart,
I was here before the fountain,
I was here from the start.'

The archaeologist did speculate
Upon what the creature claimed,
And came to the conclusion that
No conclusion could be obtained.

'I was here before all mortals,
And here before the Flood;
My lineage is ancient,
And noble is my blood.'

'Vain boaster,' said a mayfly
That was hovering around,
'Longevity is of no importance
When buried in the ground.

'On the scum of a neighbouring river
A moment ago I was born
And I am likely to vanish
Long before another dawn.

'Yet I am divinely happy
And of offspring I am sure.
I have drifted among the rosebuds,
And the sun was warm and pure.'

Mr Yi, Mr Hoi and Mr Duff

Mr Yi is very foreign,
He's always hunting yaks.
In the Himalayan mountains
Are stacks of yaks he attacks.

Mr Hoi is also foreign
He eats monkeys' brains.
He keeps their scalps upon the table
Just in case it rains
Into the monkeys' brains.

When not at home, Mr Duff
To Messrs Yi and Hoi is foreign.
They argue about what he wears
Beneath his foreign sporran.

Fashion

I dye my hair bright green,
Unless I shave it clean.
I wear a wig upon my nose
And bright earrings on my toes.
And though I know my legs are pylons
I wear such pretty nylons.
Every day upon my shirt
I dab a little grease and dirt.

(Though I'm the brightest kid in the class
And my brain is more than ample
Teacher says she thinks I'm weird
And set a bad example.)

When people stop and say,
'Why do you have that on?'
I smooth down my little dress and say,
'It is the latest fashion.'
All the girls adore me,
They do not think I'm a fool.
They smile and say, 'Our Billy's
The best-dressed boy in school.'

Enough 'Please'

I asked for the moon,
   got a slice of cheese,
Someone took it from me
   'cause I didn't say please.

Asked for firewood
   in case I should freeze,
Someone took it from me
   'cause I didn't say please.

'Please' is a word that gets
   some people in a huff.
We shouldn't have to use it
   if we only want enough.

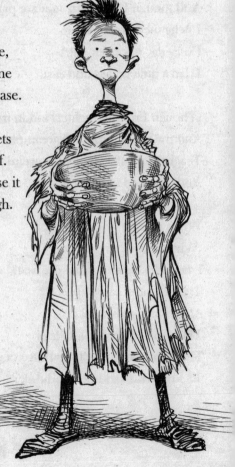

The Love-doomed Rat

Oh poor rat! Poor rat!
It's fallen in love with a cat! A cat!

Oh what will become of it?
It's hated enough for spreading plague and stuff,
It's hated enough!

It lives underground without the sun.
In its drab dark world it has no fun.

Poor rat!
The trouble it's taking to make itself clean!
It's so love-starved and lean!

I hear it say, 'My eyes are tiny
And hers are like the moon,
And soon, Oh soon I must risk it –
I must visit that cat's basket!'

What will become of it,
Struck by love to such a strange degree,
As lovesick as you or I could be?

The Fickle Promise

Sneaking close to a window-pane
A fox heard a mother vexed
Say harshly to her screaming child,
'I'll feed you to the fox!'

The fox *was* rather hungry
And the baby nice and fat;
It thought how kind the mother was
To do a thing like that.

It sat outside the window
Thinking of what the mother vowed.
It hoped the baby would scream again,
Very soon and very loud.

It did, but the mother,
Regretting what she'd said,
Murmured, 'If a fox comes, love,
We'll shoot the creature dead.'

'Ah, fickle, fickle,' said the fox,
'Very fickle that!
I will no longer drag it home,
And it was so nice and fat.'

Zonky Zizzibug

I've just appeared in this classroom,
I did not use the door.
I *have* just materialized
Through the classroom floor.

Do not call *me* a liar.
Do not call *me* a cheat.
No, teacher cannot see me,
Sitting in this seat.

My name *is* Zonky Zizzibug.
I don't know why you laugh.
This book is not a comic,
It's an extraterrestrial graph.

I don't care what you say.
Oh please don't be a bore!
I *did* just materialize.
I did *not* use the door.

I have an anti-matter,
Anti-gravity device.
I also have a pill
For turning schoolboys into mice.

Do not call me a liar.
Do not call me a cheat.
You are not imagining things.
Do not blame the heat.

I *have* been to Venus.
I *have* been to Mars.
I've even been to Uranus
And several other stars.

Of course my blood is green!
The aerial on my head?
Oh that's just something
That stops me being dead.

How dare you laugh and scoff!
Shush. Everyone will hear.
Look, teacher's giving you
A *very* funny stare.

I *won't* say I'm Zonky Zizzibug.
I *am* going to go away.
I'm only allowed to play on earth
For a single day.

I'm going to drift around the classroom.
I'm going to float up in the air.
Then I'm going back off home
Because laughing is not fair.

I won't become visible.
I won't float down from the shelf.
I do not care if teacher
Thinks you are talking to yourself.

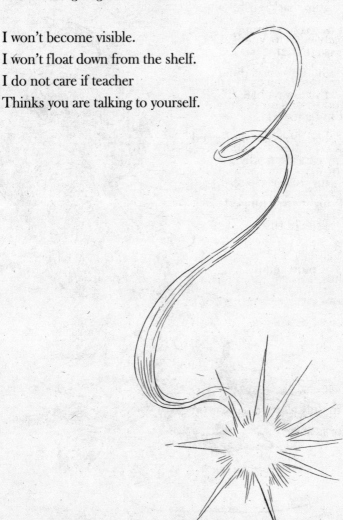

A Dog's Life

Sigh, sob,
   gulp, bark, gush,
I'm soggy, swampy,
   saturated,
bathtime's something
   I've always hated!
I'm bedewed,
   bedabbled, waterlogged,
my ears are frothy,
   my dose is clogged,
I might grow fungus!
   I might rust!
Bathing a dog
   is most unjust!

Uncle Right and Uncle Wrong

Uncle
Right said
he knew the
right way to build
a boat. Uncle Wrong was
convinced it would never float.
'Wrong,' said Right, 'please don't gloat.
I'm sure this boy would like to float in a super-
fabulous fan-terrific boat.' 'If he did,' said Wrong,
'he'd rue the day. Before he could blink, that boat would
sink.'

T
h
e
y

quibbled and they squabbled and I'd heard it all before, so I built
my own boat and sailed from the seashore, while Uncle
Right and Uncle Wrong argued bitterly (though they
stopped at lunchtime and sometimes during tea).

The Ass in a Lion's Skin

Dressed up in a lion's skin
An ass, far from bright,
Caused terror to its master
And gave everyone a fright.

Dressed up, it felt important
As it sneaked out late at night
To terrorize the neighbourhood
While it wasn't very light.

One day the ass's master
Threw away his fears.
Sticking through the lion's skin
He saw the ass's ears.

'Stupid creature!' yelled its master,
'Stupid! Dumb! Daft!'
He hit the ass with great relief,
But was nervous when he laughed.

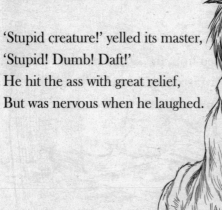

Pick-a-nose Pick

Pick-a-nose pick-a-nose pick-a-nose Pick
Picked his nose and made me sick.
Pick-a-nose pick-a-nose pick-a-nose Pick
Picks his nose very quick.
Pick-a-nose pick-a-nose pick-a-nose Pick
Gets rid of it with one fast flick.
Flick flick flick flick flick
Pick-a-nose pick-a-nose makes me sick.

Pick-a-nose Pick's Awful Poem

A tadpole doesn't have much snot in its nose
But a whale has got a lot of snot I suppose.
Snot! Snot! Green slimy snot!
I like it a lot!

You can slip on it in the dark,
And spread it on bread for a lark.
Snot! Snot! Green slimy snot!
I like it a lot!

I think you will agree
There's not much snot in a flea.
Snot! Snot! Green and hot!
I like it a lot!

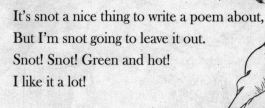

It's snot a nice thing to write a poem about,
But I'm snot going to leave it out.
Snot! Snot! Green and hot!
I like it a lot!

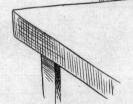

'It's Time for Bed, You Know'

When I'm desperate to find the answer
To something I do not know
Mum says, 'Ask your father.'
He says, 'It's time for bed, you know.'

'Why does the world spin so slow?'
'It's time for bed, you know.'

'Why don't fireflies always glow?'
'It's time for bed, you know.'

'Why don't owls or pigeons crow?'
'It's time for bed, you know.'

I went to a library,
Picked a book called *Learn and Grow.*
Just when I chose to open it
Dad winked, 'It's time for bed, you know.'

There must be a better ploy
For staying up late to see
The movies I'm not supposed to watch
On video and TV . . .

Feeding the Family

Frog-spawn pie! Frog-spawn pie!
When I feed it to my sister
It makes her cry.

Custard and fish! Custard and fish!
When I feed it to my brother
He's sick in his dish.

Slug-and-worm jam! Slug-and-worm jam!
When I feed it to the baby
It jumps out of the pram.

Garlic jelly! Garlic jelly!
When I feed it to my father
His breath goes smelly.

Rice and rat! Rice and rat!
When I feed it to my mother
She's sick on the cat.

I want to be an astronaut!
I want to write a book!
I don't want to be a ballerina,
Or a cook!

Why Grump?

Mr Thrump had a stump
where his knee should be,
and though he never grumped he stumped
about continually.

He thought, 'Why grump about this stump
when it's plain for all to see,
those who stump and grump end in a dump
while I am full of glee.'

The Vampire's Off His Blood

I love sneaking into horror films,
They're frightening but fun,
And when I go to bed at night
I don't need a special gun.

The vampire in the cupboard,
The werewolf beneath the bed,
The poltergeist in the night-lamp
Are scared of me instead!

The reason is very simple,
It is not because I'm brave,
But they're frightened of little boys
Who come back from the grave.

When I walk into my room at night
This is what I pretend.
The poltergeist gets so scared
It sends him round the bend.

Now the vampire's off his blood
And prefers thick clotted cream.
The werewolf now likes nursery rhymes
And is afraid to scream.

I've never seen them once
But still I sit and moan,
I growl very grisly ghastly growls
So they'll leave me on my own.

What Happened to Miss Frugle

Stern Miss Frugle always said
To Peter and his sister,
'After school you'll stay behind
If you so much as whisper.'

Then one winter afternoon
While skating on thin ice,
The children saw it crack and Miss
Frugle vanish in a trice.

People wondered where she'd gone,
But no one really missed her,
And she was never found because
Peter and his sister

didn't so much as whisper
didn't so much as whisper.

The Tree and the Pool

'I don't want my leaves to drop,' said the tree.
'I don't want to freeze,' said the pool.
'I don't want to smile,' said the sombre man.
'Or ever to cry,' said the Fool.

'I don't want to open,' said the bud.
'I don't want to end,' said the night.
'I don't want to rise,' said the neap-tide.
'Or ever to fall,' said the kite.

They wished and they murmured and whispered,
They said that to change was a crime,
Then a voice from nowhere answered,
'You must do what I say,' said Time.

The Frogologist

I hate it when grown-ups say,
'What do you want to be?'
I hate the way they stand up there
And talk down to me.

I say:

'I want to be a frogologist
And study the lives of frogs,
I want to know their habitat
And crawl about in bogs,
I want to learn to croak and jump
And catch flies with my tongue
And will they please excuse me 'cause
Frogologists start quite young.'

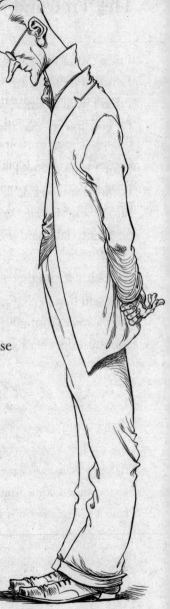

Index of First Lines